THIS BOOK
BELONGS TO

Patrick
Hetherington

By the Same Author

SELBY'S SIDE-SPLITTING JOKE BOOK

DUNCAN BALL

illustrated by Allan Stomann

Angus&Robertson
An imprint of HarperCollins*Publishers*

Acknowledgments from the author: Many thanks once again to the team at HarperCollins, Australia, especially Vanessa Radnidge and Peter Guo. Also thanks to Amanda O'Connell and, as always, to Allan Stomann.

Angus&Robertson

An imprint of HarperCollins*Publishers*, Australia

First published in Australia in 2002
by HarperCollins*Publishers* Pty Limited
ABN 36 009 913 517
A member of the HarperCollins*Publishers* (Australia) Pty Limited Group
www. harpercollins.com.au

Text compilation copyright © Duncan Ball 2002
Illustrations copyright © Allan Stomann 2002

HarperCollins*Publishers*
25 Ryde Road, Pymble, Sydney, NSW 2073, Australia
31 View Road, Glenfield, Auckland 10, New Zealand
77–85 Fulham Palace Road, London W6 8JB, United Kingdom
Hazelton Lanes, 55 Avenue Road, Suite 2900, Toronto, Ontario M5R 3L2
and 1995 Markham Road, Scarborough, Ontario M1B 5M8, Canada
10 East 53rd Street, New York NY 10022, USA

National Library of Australia Cataloguing-in-Publication data:

Ball, Duncan, 1941– .
   Selby's side-splitting joke book.
   ISBN 0 207 19853 5.
   1. Australian wit and humour – Juvenile fiction.
   I. Stomann, Allan. II. Title.
A828.302

Printed and bound in Australia by Griffin Press on 80gsm Econoprint

5 4 3 2 1   02 03 04 05

'Waste no time in reading this book.'

— Gary Gaggs

AUTHOR'S NOTE

Those who know the Selby books, will know that he is the only talking dog in Australia and, perhaps, the world and that he rings me up and tells me stories about himself which I dutifully record. There are now ten such books of stories about him, plus a book of selected stories called, *Selby's Selection*, and one previous joke book called *Selby's Joke Book*.

Gary Gaggs is a stand-up comedian from the town Selby lives in and which Selby calls, 'Bogusville'. He is one of the funniest funnymen in the history of the Australian bush. Once at a nursing home the old people laughed so hard that by the end of his show, Gary was knee-deep in false teeth. That was one of Gary's proudest moments.

Gary has also been called a comic vacuum cleaner because of the way he sucks up everyone else's jokes and then retells them. He loves mouldy old jokes and no one can tell them the way he does. He used to make up some of his own jokes but stopped after a terrifying experience. It happened one night at the Bogusville Bijou Theatre when Gary told the joke that became known as his 'killer joke'. The joke was so funny that the audience couldn't stop laughing. Gary had to stop his show as people were rushed to hospital with all manner of laughter-related injuries. Some of them didn't stop laughing till they got their medical bills a week later. Gary has never dared tell this joke again. I've never heard it so it's not in this collection. But I hope you like the jokes that are here.

Duncan Ball

CONTENTS

SERIOUSLY, FOLKS

Gary Gagge is such a funny guy
and this book is filled with his
jokes. He's the sort of funnyman
who never tells the same joke twice.
In fact, if he tells a joke once, he
tells it again and again and again —
but never just twice. But seriously,
folks, I love this guy and I love
his jokes. I don't care where he
got them. I hope you don't either.

So if you're sad
If you're feeling blue
Here's a gaggle of gags
From Gary to you.

I hope you love them as much as I do!

Selby

a Gaggle of Gags

HA HA!

A mother centipede said to her baby, 'It's time to turn out the lights now and go to sleep.' The baby centipede said, 'Can't we play "This Little Piggy" one more time?'

A nervous balloon went up to a pin and said, 'Hello, buster.'

A duck walked into a chemist shop and said, 'Do you have any lipstick?' The chemist said, 'Certainly. Would you like to pay for that now?' And the duck said, 'No, just put it on my bill.'

A boy stayed up all night wondering where the sun had gone. Finally it dawned on him.

A grandmother asked her granddaughter, 'Do you like raisin toast, dear?' And the granddaughter said, 'I don't know, I've never raised any.'

A fish swam into a concrete wall and said, 'Dam!'

The art teacher said to the student, 'What's that you're drawing?'
'That's me being chased by a bear.'
'But all I see is the bear,' the teacher said.
'I got away,' said the student.

Two mosquitoes were looking at a camel. One of the mosquitoes said, 'Hey, did I do that?'

A rope went into a restaurant and the waiter said, 'Get out of here. We don't serve ropes in here.' The rope went out, tied itself up and dragged itself along the footpath. Then it went back to the restaurant and the waiter said, 'I told you that we don't serve ropes here.' The rope said, 'But I'm not a rope.' 'You're not?' said the waiter. The rope said, 'No, I'm a frayed knot.'

A boatload of shoes hit a reef and sank. Three hundred soles were lost at sea.

A boy found an old brass lamp and rubbed it. A genie came out granting him one wish. 'I want to be irresistible to girls,' the boy said. *Poof!* The genie turned him into a fluffy kitten.

Two hungry cannibals wandered through the rainforest and found a couple of people sleeping in sleeping-bags. 'Look,' the first one said, 'breakfast in bed.'

A bee was waiting at a buzz stop.

A ghost teacher was teaching her class how to walk through walls. One of the girl ghosts said, 'I'm sorry, Miss, but I just don't get it.' 'All right,' the teacher said. 'Look at the blackboard and I'll go through it one more time.'

An ant ran across the top of a packet of peanuts. Another ant said, 'Why did you do that?' 'Because,' answered the first ant, 'it says, "To open, tear across the dotted line".'

A ball was rolling down a hill. Finally it stopped and looked round.

A man went to a very posh restaurant and the owner said, 'I'm sorry, sir, but you can't come in here without a tie.' So the man went back to his car, got the jumper leads out of the boot and tied one of them around his neck in a bow. He went back to the restaurant and said, 'Can I come in now?' The owner said, 'Certainly, sir — but just don't try to start anything.'

A girl really wanted to see a flying saucer so she tripped a waiter.

'Daddy, will you put a nail through my hula hoop?'
    'Why would you want me to do that?'
    'I want to turn it into a navel destroyer.'

A duck went into a supermarket and said, 'Do you have any duck food? Where's the duck food? I want some duck food.'

The manager came out and said, 'I'm sorry but we don't have any duck food.'

'I want some duck food!' the duck yelled.

'We don't have any!' the manager said. 'And we don't serve ducks, so please leave.'

The duck came back the next day and said, 'I know you've got duck food — now where is it?'

The manager said, 'I told you before and I'll tell you again, we don't have any! Now if you don't get out of here, I'll nail your feet to the floor!'

The duck came back the next day and the manager was standing in the doorway.

The duck looked around nervously and then said, 'Do you have any nails?'

'No, we don't,' said the manager.

'Then do you have any duck food?' the duck asked.

ridiculous riddles

What do you call a dog with a sore throat?
A husky.

What do you do when you see two snails fighting?
Let them slug it out.

Why do hairdressers make good taxi drivers?
They know all the short-cuts.

Why did the harpist sell her harp very cheaply?
There were no strings attached.

What do you call a handicrafts teacher?
A real sew-and-sew.

What is black and white and red all over?
A baby magpie with nappy rash.

What did the girl say to the Maths book?
'Boy, do you have problems.'

What kind of sneakers do chickens run around in?

Re bok bok bok.

What do you call a donkey with three legs?

A wonkey.

What happened to the dog who swallowed a watch?

He got ticks.

What do you call a lot of rabbits hopping away from you?

A receding hareline.

What does an octopus wear to stay warm in cold water?

A coat of arms.

How do hens and roosters dance?

Chick to chick.

How do you stop a skunk from smelling?

Hold its nose.

What kind of books do skunks read?

Best-smellers.

What grows on trees and is terrified of wolves?

The three little figs.

What do frogs ask for in restaurants?

French flies.

Where do sheep go to get their hair cut?

   The baa baas.

Where do bunnies go after their wedding?

   On a bunny-moon.

Why is it expensive to keep pelicans?

   Because you're faced with some large bills.

What do cows eat for breakfast?

   Moo-slie.

Why is it that anteaters rarely get sick?

Because they're full of anty bodies.

What do you call a parrot wearing a raincoat?

Polyunsaturated.

What kind of car do dogs like best?

A Pawsche.

What did the leopard say after dinner?

'That certainly hit the spots.'

Why didn't the frog drown when she fell in the water?

Because it was only *knee-deep, knee-deep, knee-deep.*

Why didn't the piglets let their father tell them bedtime stories?

Because he was a boar.

What animal do you look like when you get in the bath?

A little bear.

What happened when the police questioned the duck?

It quacked under pressure.

What did the grape say when the elephant sat on it?

Nothing. It just let out a little w(h)ine.

Knock Knock Once

Don't knock
these jokes!

Knock knock.
Who's there?
Dwayne.
Dwayne who?
Dwayne the bath! I'm dwowning!

Knock knock.
Who's there?
Robin.
Robin who?
I'm Robin you, so hand over your money!

Knock knock.
Who's there?
Ken.
Ken who?
Ken you just open the door?

Knock knock.
Who's there?
Amos.
Amos who?
A mosquito.

I think I heard the buzzer!

Knock knock.
Who's there?
An author.
An author who?
Another mosquito.

Knock knock.
Who's there?
Yetta.
Yetta who?
Yettanother mosquito.

Knock knock.
Who's there?
Mandy.
Mandy who?
Man de lifeboats! We're sinking!

Knock knock.
Who's there?
Ivor.
Ivor who?
Ivor cold bum from waiting outside so long, let me in!

Knock knock.
Who's there?
Little old lady.
Little old lady who?
I didn't know you could yodel.

Knock knock.
Who's there?
Abba.
Abba who?
Abba good weekend!

Knock knock.
Who's there?
Sienna.
Sienna who?
Sienna good movies recently?

Knock knock.
Who's there?
Abel.
Abel who?
A bell would save me having to knock.

Knock knock.
Who's there?
Frankfurter.
Frankfurter who?
Frankfurter lovely evening.

Knock knock.
Who's there?
Dexter.
Dexter who?
Dexter halls with boughs of holly, fa-la-la-la-la-la-la-la-la.

Knock knock.
Who's there?
Fortification.
Fortification who?
Fortification we're going to the Gold Coast.

Knock knock.
Who's there?
Sonia.
Sonia who?
Sonia shoe — and it stinks!

Knock knock.
Who's there?
Dewey.
Dewey who?
Dewey have to listen to all these knock knock jokes?

I Hate

Restaurants!

**A stand-up comedy routine
by Gary Gaggs**

Every time I go into a restaurant I have trouble. I always get these smartypants waiters. Last night it was the same. As soon as I approached my table I knew I'd made a big mistake. There was a cigarette butt on the floor and I said to the waiter, 'Excuse me, but is that yours?' And he said, 'No, it's all yours. You saw it first.'

I said, 'Do you serve crabs?' And he said, 'We'll serve anyone. Just sit down.'

I looked at the menu and I said, 'Do you have asparagus?' And he said, 'No, I don't have a sparrow and please don't call me Gus.' That's what he said.

I said, 'I think I'd like some chips.' And he said, 'I'm sorry but it's not *fry*-day.'

So I ordered some soup and I waited and waited and waited. Finally I called the waiter over and said, 'I've been waiting for my soup for over an hour!' And he said, 'I'm sorry, sir, but the chef was out having dinner.'

Finally he brought a bowl of soup but he had his thumb in it. I said, 'Listen here now, you've got your thumb in my soup!' And he said, 'Don't worry — it's not very hot.'

I had a spoonful and then I said, 'This soup tastes funny.' And he said, 'Then why aren't you laughing?'

I said, 'Seriously, what is this?' And he said, 'It's bean soup, sir.' So I said, 'I don't care what it's been, what is it now?'

Then I said, 'Look, there's a dead cockroach floating in it!' And he said, 'Yes, I'm afraid they're terrible swimmers.'

I said, 'And there's a bee in it, too.' And he said, 'Then I must have given you the alphabet soup.'

I said, 'This is dreadful! Get me the manager!' And the waiter said, 'Save your breath, he won't eat it either.'

I said, 'Take it away! Get me a baked potato and step on it!' Guess what? He did.

Then I ordered some roast tongue and when he brought it out he had his hand on it. I said, 'Will you please get your hand off my food?!' And he said, 'I'm terribly sorry, sir, but I just didn't want it to fall on the floor again.'

So he let go of it and it fell on the tablecloth. He picked it up, put it back on the plate and said, 'Sorry, just a slip of the tongue.'

I said, 'This meal isn't fit for a pig!' And he said, 'If you'll just be patient, sir, I'll get you one that is.'

I said, 'And, by the way, what do I have to do to get a glass of water around here?' And the waiter said, 'Well, you could always try setting yourself on fire.' That's what he said. What an idiot.

I said, 'I think I'll have some fish.' So he brought me out this awful-looking fish. I said, 'This smells off.' And he said, 'Long time, no *sea*.'

I said, 'It doesn't even look like it's been cleaned.' And he said, 'Why would you clean a fish that's been in water all its life?'

I said, 'But I thought it was going to be battered?' Suddenly he screamed, 'Take that!' and he hit it with his fist. 'Now it's battered,' he said.

'Forget the main course,' I said. 'What do you have for dessert? Can you make an apple puff?' And he said, 'Certainly, sir, I'll just chase one around the table.'

I said, 'Seriously, do you know how to make a blueberry twirl?' And he said, 'Personally, I'd send it to ballet school.'

Finally I decided on apple crumble with ice cream on top. When he

brought it I said, 'This is the saddest apple crumble I've ever seen!' And he said, 'Oh, I'm terribly sorry, sir, I thought you asked for apple *grumble.*'

And I said, 'What's that fly doing on the ice cream?' And he said, 'I think it's skiing.'

I said, 'Take it away! Do you have any trifle?' And he said, 'We did but it was taken into *custardy.*' I kid you not, that's exactly what he said.

I said, 'Do you have any doughnuts?' And he said, 'I'm sorry but the chef is fed up with the *hole* business.'

Thanks, folks, you were great! I'd take you out to dinner anytime — but maybe to a different restaurant.

a Giggle of Gaggles

HE HEE!

A bee flew back to his hive and said, 'Honey, I'm home.'

A frog came limping into an animal hospital and said, 'I need a hopperation.' (When it was over he felt hoppy again.)

A teacher said to the class, 'Just imagine that you are back in the time of the dinosaurs. You're playing with a cute little baby Tyrannosaurus when suddenly its mother comes over the hill. What would you do?'

A voice at the back of the room said, 'I'd stop imagining!'

A young bat set off for school but came home soon after. She said to her mother, 'The bus didn't come.' The mother bat said, 'Maybe you didn't hang around long enough.'

It was Saturday afternoon and a herd of cows went to the moooooovies.

One of the cows was walking backwards. She said, 'Oom oom.'

To encourage the kids to wash their hands, the principal put a sign over the handbasins in the toilets that said THINK! The next day someone had written next to it: THOAP!

A little cannibal was eating dinner. He said, 'Daddy, I hate my teacher's guts.' His father said, 'Well, then just eat around them.'

Two spiders were riding in a car that said, 'Just Married' on the back. Another spider called out, 'Hey, look at the newlywebs!'

'Mum, Mum, throw me that fish!'
'But, darling, I'm about to cook it.'
'I know, but I never caught a fish before.'

Where do magpies go shopping? At a swoopermarket.

A woman took her cat to the vet. She said, 'I've been leaving my spare change in a bowl in the kitchen and it keeps disappearing. I think my cat's eating it.' The vet X-rayed the cat and said, 'You're right, there's money in the kitty.'

'Would you come to my birthday party on Saturday?' a girl asked one of her classmates. 'Well, yes. Where do you live?' the other girl asked. 'I live at 22 Pine Street. Just knock on the door with your elbow.' 'With my elbow? Why with my elbow?' 'Well, I hope you're not coming empty-handed.'

Did you hear about the little cat who wanted to work at the animal hospital? She wanted to be a first-aid kit.

A man went into a cafe with a frog on his head and the waiter said, 'Where'd you get that?' And the frog said, 'I don't know, it started out as a little bump on my bottom.'

Another man went into a cafe wearing a beret and the waiter said, 'Hey, cool, where'd you get that?' and the beret said, 'France — they've got millions of them there.'

A boy was so stupid that once he went to a mind-reader and the woman gave him his money back.

A vacuum cleaner salesperson came to the door and said to the woman who opened it, 'Buy one of these and it'll cut your work in half.'
'Good,' the woman said, 'I'll take two of them.'

A boy drowned in a bowl of muesli. A currant pulled him under.

A caveman and a cavewoman were eating roast mammoth with their children. Suddenly a small meteor streaked down and crashed to the ground next to them. A cave boy picked it up, popped it in his mouth and ate it. His mother screamed, 'Why did you do that?! What's wrong with the food I made?!' And the boy said, 'Sorry, Mum, but that was a little meteor.'

Miss Bonzer's *beaut* books

READ MORE BOOKS!

How to Win Arguments with Your School Librarian by Xavier Breth

How I Outran a Bear by Claude Bottom

Police Questioning by Howard I. Knowe

He Loves Me by Mae B. Soh

Gambling Made Easy by Jack Pot

Cooking with Dirt by I. M. Strange

I Can't Walk Another Step by Carrie Mee Holme

Locked in a Prison by Dora Steele

Sadness by I. M. Blue

Bring Your Pocket Money by Justin Case

The Toothache by O. Howard Hertz

The Angry Lioness by Sheila Tacke

I Shot a Lioness by Mr Completely

The Butler's Secret by E. Dunnett

Surgery for Beginners by Caesar Hart

Building a House by Iva Newhouse

The Self-Made Millionaire by Jonah Lott

Winter Mountaineering by I. C. Snow

Attack on the Aquarium by Freda Wales

Police Chase by Watts E. Dunn

Close the Curtain by I. C. Hugh

Plumbing for Beginners by Lee King

Gary Gaggs: The Greatest Comedian
by Jess Joe King

The Liquid Diet by I. P. Allott

name
Shame

What do you call a girl who gets up at sunset? Eve.

What do you call a man lying on a doorstep? Matt

What do you call a woman with one leg shorter than the other? Eileen

What do you call a woman lying in the middle of a tennis court? Annette

What do you call a boy with short hair? Shawn

What do you call a nutty girl? Hazel

What do you call a boy carrying a toilet? Lou

What do you call a girl carrying two toilets? Lulu

What do you call a lion tamer? Claude

What do you call someone who's been nailed to a wall? Art

What do you call a girl with one foot on one side of a stream and one foot on the other? Bridget

What do you call a naked man? Seymour

What do you call a gravedigger? Doug

What do you call a gravedigger on his lunch-break? Douglas

What do you call a man floating in the sea? Bob

What do you call a woman climbing a wall? Ivy

What do you call a woman who is far away? Dot

What do you call a mountaineer? Cliff

Hi Jack! Can you give me a lift?

What do you call a man lifting a car? Jack

What do you call an auto mechanic? Axel

What do you call a bodybuilder? Jim

What do you call a girl who loves honey? Bea

What do you call a florist? Blossom

What do you call a rodeo rider? Buck

What do you call a sweet little girl? Candy

What do you call a girl giving a boy a piggyback? Carrie

What do you call a boy giving a girl a piggyback? Carter

What do you call a thief? Rob

What do you call a woman with a wooden leg? Peg

What do you call someone who hasn't paid you back? Owen

What do you call a boy who is a long way away? Miles

What do you call a boy with leaves in his underpants? Russell

Insults and Injuries

If brains were dynamite, you wouldn't have enough to blow your nose.

If I threw a stick, would you leave?

I wouldn't know what to do without you, but let's find out.

The next time you pass my house — I'll be very happy.

Haven't I met you before? Or was it just a nightmare?

Why don't you blow your brains out? You've got nothing to lose.

If I've said anything to insult you, please believe me, it was on purpose.

I never forget a face — but in your case I'll try my best.

I wish you were a distant relative. The more distant the better.

Don't go away. I want to forget you just the way you are.

For a second I didn't recognise you. It was the best second of my life.

I feel sorry for your brain — it must be lonely in that big head of yours.

The last time I saw a face like yours I fed it a banana.

You've only got two faults: everything you say and everything you do.

Why don't you go to the swimming pool and have some drowning lessons?

Your bus is leaving soon. Be under it.

You have good mechanical skills. But when your mouth is in gear, your mind is in neutral.

Tell me everything you know — I've got a minute to spare.

Have you ever thought of hiring yourself out to haunt houses?

Is that your head, or is your neck blowing bubblegum?

Surely you were given that nose of yours so you could breathe and keep your mouth shut.

I'll say this for you: you're not two-faced. If you were, you wouldn't be wearing that one.

Every time you walk by a girl, she sighs — with relief.

You've got such a big mouth, you could sing a duet — by yourself.

You're so dumb that you probably think that barnacles are where they keep seahorses.

That car of yours is so old it's a wonder it doesn't have Roman numerals on its numberplates.

You've got such a big mouth you could eat a banana sideways.

Don't let your mind wander — it's not strong enough to go out on its own.

Let's go to the dress-up party as a horse. I'll be the front end and you just be yourself.

Looks aren't everything. In your case, they aren't anything.

You've got a very sympathetic face. What a face — you've got my sympathy.

Knock
and Knock
again

Knock knock.
Who's there?
Armageddon.
Armageddon who?
Armageddon outta here!

Knock knock.
Who's there?
Attila.
Attila who?
Attila you no lies if you ask me no questions.

Knock knock.
Who's there?
Aurora.
Aurora who?
Aurora's just come from an angry lion.

Knock knock.
Who's there?
Cattle.
Cattle who?
Cattle purr if you
pat it.

Knock knock.
Who's there?
Augusta.
Augusta who?
Augusta wind will blow your house down.

Knock knock.
Who's there?
Meg.
Meg who?
Meg it quick and open the door.

Knock knock.
Who's there?
Wilfred.
Wilfred who?
Wilfred come out to play?

Knock knock.
Who's there?
Annette.
Annette who?
Annette curtain would look nice in your window.

Knock knock.
Who's there?
Aitch.
Aitch who?
Bless you!

Knock knock.
Who's there?
Adair.
Adair who?
Adair you to open the door.

Knock knock.
Who's there?
Adair.
Adair who?
Adair once but now I'm bald.

Knock knock.
Who's there?
Adam.
Adam who?
Adam up and give me the total.

Knock knock.
Who's there?
Abbey.
Abbey who?
Abbey just stung me on the bottom!

Knock knock.
Who's there?
Noah.
Noah who?
No accounting for taste.

Knock knock.
Who's there?
Delta.
Delta who?
Delta great hand in a card game last night.

Knock knock.
Who's there?
Marcella.
Marcella who?
Marcella's underwater and mah house's about to float away!

Knock knock.
Who's there?
Saul.
Saul who?
Saul there is — there isn't any more.

Knock knock.
Who's there?
Quacker.
Quacker who?
Quacker 'nother knock knock joke and I'm leaving!

Double
Crosses

Can you
guess what
you'll get?

What do you get when you cross a duck with a rooster?

A bird that wakes you up at the quack of dawn.

What do you get if you cross a chicken with a bomb?

An eggs-plosion.

What do you get if you cross a skunk with a teddy?

Pooh Bear.

What do you get when you cross a male cat with a sparrow?

A peeping Tom.

What do you get if you cross a robber with a cement mixer?

A hardened criminal.

What do you get when you cross a robber with a chicken?

A peck-pocket.

What do you get if you cross a teacher with a vampire?

I don't know but it gives lots of blood tests.

What do you get if you cross a boomerang with a bad memory?

I can't remember but I'm sure it will come back to me.

What do you get if you cross a crocodile with a camera?

A snapshot.

What do you get if you cross a rooster with a poodle?

Cock-a-poodle-do!

What do you get if you cross a rooster, a poodle, and a ghost?

Cock-a-poodle-boo!

What do you get if you cross a boomerang with a bad Christmas present?

A gift that returns itself.

What do you get if you cross two snakes with a magician?

Addercadabra and abradacobra.

What do you get if you cross a brumby with a dog?

An animal whose buck is worse than its bite.

What do you get if you cross a piranha with a parrot?

A fish that'll talk your head off.

What do you get if you cross a toad with a galaxy?

Star Warts.

What do you get if you cross a praying mantis with a termite?

An insect that says grace before eating your house.

What do you get if you cross a centipede with a parrot?

A walkie-talkie.

What do you get if you cross a rabbit with a flea?

Bugs Bunny.

What do you get if you cross a mouse with an orange?

A pip-squeak.

What do you get if you cross a tiger with a snowman?

Frostbite.

What do you get if you cross a boy scout with a monster?

A creature that scares little old ladies across the road.

What do you get if you cross a cow with an octopus?

An animal that can milk itself.

What do you get if you cross a monkey with a skunk?

King Pong.

What do you get if you cross King Kong with a kangaroo?

Big holes in the ground.

What do you get if you cross a big gorilla with a cement-mixer?

King Kongcrete.

What do you get if you cross the Easter Bunny with a parrot?

An animal that tells you where it hid the eggs.

What do you get if you cross a sheepdog with a rose?

A cauliflower.

Why did the couple get engaged while double-bungy-jumping?

They wanted to be heels over head in love.

What do you get if you cross an owl with a comet?

A hooting star.

What do you get if you cross a centipede with a chicken?

Enough drumsticks for everyone.

What do you get when you cross a werewolf with a drip-dry suit?

A wash-and-werewolf.

Sick
Again

A stand-up comedy routine
by Gary Gaggs

I felt sick again this morning so I decided to go to the doctor. I said to the doctor, 'Every morning I feel sick for the first half-hour after I get up.' And she said, 'Then get up half an hour later.' That's what she said.

I said, 'Honestly, Doctor, I feel like I just crawled out of a garbage bin.' And she said, 'Don't talk rubbish!'

I said, 'But I'm as sick as a dog.' And she said, 'How long have you been feeling this way?' And I said, 'Ever since I was a pup.'

That's not what I really said. I said, 'I snore so much I wake myself up.' And she said, 'Have you tried sleeping in another room?'

I said, 'I took some medicine for it but I accidentally swallowed the spoon.' And she said, 'I'll try not to stir you up.'

Did you hear about the guy who tiptoed past the medicine cabinet? He didn't want to wake the *sleeping* pills. (I always loved that one!)

I said, 'But you don't understand, I keep hallucinating.' And the doctor said, 'You're just imagining it.'

I said, 'I feel like I'm at death's door.' And she said, 'Don't worry, I'll pull you through.'

I said, 'But Doctor, I feel like I could be dead in sixty seconds.' 'Hold on,' she said, 'I'll be with you in a minute.'

Anyway, I said to the doctor, 'I think I'm going to die!' And she said, 'Don't worry, I'll give you some coffin medicine.'

I said, 'I haven't been feeling well since my operation.' She said, 'What operation?' And I said,

'Last month they took out my appendix, my gall bladder, my adenoids and my tonsils.' And she said, 'That's enough out of you!'

She said, 'Did you eat anything that you think might have made you sick?' And I said that I had roast duck last night. So she said, 'That explains why you're *down* in the mouth.'

I said, 'I didn't eat the down but I did eat a kilo of dried fruit, ten eggs and a whole stick of butter.' And she said, 'What a fruitcake!'

I said, 'But you don't understand, it gave me wind.' And she said, 'Then why don't you buy a kite?'

I said, 'There's a ringing in my ear.' And she said, 'Have you tried answering it?'

I said, 'My life is becoming a joke.' And she said, 'Don't make me laugh!'

I said, 'Everyone wants to argue with me.' And she said, 'They do not!'

I said, 'Everyone calls me a liar.' And she said, 'I find that hard to believe.'

I said, 'But you don't understand. No one ever listens to what I have to say.' And she yelled out, 'Next!'

I said, 'Doctor, this is serious. I think I have a cold. What would you take for this cold?' And she said, 'Make me an offer.'

I said, 'My throat is sore and my voice is getting raspy. I'm beginning to sound like Donald Duck.' And she said, 'You're probably just having a Disney spell.'

I said, 'You're not helping me. I'm sure it's a cold because my nose is starting to run.' And she said, 'Quick! Take this rope and tie it up!'

I said, 'If I keep losing weight, I'll be invisible.' And she said, 'Who said that?'

I said, 'Everything's wrong with me. I think one of my teeth has grown in backwards.' And she said, 'Ahah! So that's what's eating you.'

She said, 'Okay, I'm going to give you a prescription for some little blue, green and yellow glass balls.' And I said, 'What do I do with those?' And she said, 'Swallow them and you'll feel *marbleous.*'

I said, 'Why are you writing the prescription on my ankle?' And she said, 'Don't worry about that, it's just a footnote.'

I was getting nowhere with this doctor so I jumped on her back and yelled out, 'One, two, three, four!' She yelled back, 'Get off me! What do you think you're doing?' And I said, 'I always knew I could count on you.'

And that's what happened when I went to the doctor. Thanks, folks, you're beautiful!

A
Waggle of
Wags

These are hysterical!

A cat was watching a video. Suddenly it pressed the paws button.

The mother kangaroo was unhappy because it was raining and the kids had to play inside.

A woman went into a department store and asked the sales clerk, 'Do you carry pianos?' And the clerk said, 'No, I've got a bad back.'

A chicken went into a library and said, '*Book*.' The librarian said, 'Do you want to borrow a book? Is that it?' The librarian got a book and the chicken walked out with it. The next day the chicken returned the book and said, '*Book-book*.' And the librarian said, 'Oh, so you want to borrow two books.' The librarian got two books off the shelf and the chicken walked out with them. On the third day the chicken said, '*Book-book-book*,' and took out three books. The librarian had to know what was going on so he followed the chicken to a pond where it showed the books to a frog. The frog said, '*Redit redit redit*.'

Two frogs went for the same fly at the same time and got tongue-tied.

A French farm boy came into the barn to milk the cows and his father said, 'Where were you? What took you so long?' And the boy said, 'I was crossing the cow paddock  and my beret blew off. I had to try on twenty of them before I found the right one.'

A sick chicken had to go home from school. She had people pox.

A cannibal boy asked his mother, 'Mum, can I eat roast lamb with my fingers?' And his mother said, 'No, son, I'd eat them separately if I were you.'

A mother dog took her baby dog to a doctor dog and said, 'Doctor, Doctor, my baby is burning up with fever!' The doctor dog said, 'Quick! Put tomato sauce on him. It's good for hot dogs.'

A woman went to a funeral parlour and said, 'My pet elephant died. Could you bury him?' And the funeral director said, 'But that's a huge undertaking.'

A girl was telling a boy about the seaside town where her family goes on holidays. 'That place is so boring.' she said, 'that the tide went out and never came in again.'

A lion cub was chasing a hunter around a tree. The lion cub's mother said, 'How many times do I have to tell you? Don't play with your food!'

A mother turkey was scolding her children. 'If your father could see you now,' she said, 'he'd turn over in his gravy!'

A man was talking to a friend. 'I used to have a flea circus,' he said. 'Really?' said his friend. 'What happened?' The man said, 'A dog came along and stole the whole show.'

A doctor was examining a patient. The doctor said, 'Now breathe out very slowly.' 'Do you want to check my lungs?' the patient asked. 'No,' said the doctor, 'I just want to clean my glasses.'

'Okay,' a mother said to her son, 'if you fall out of that tree and break your legs, don't come running to me.'

A boy was going back to his seat in a darkened movie theatre and he said to the woman on the aisle, 'Did I step on your toes when I went out?' 'You most certainly did!' the woman said. 'Good,' said the boy, 'then I must be in the right row.'

A girl said, 'Mum, are you a light sleeper?' And her mother said, 'No, dear, I sleep in the dark.'

One hundred hares escaped from a rabbit farm. The police combed the area.

A girl said to her mother, 'I can't stand broccoli and I'm glad I can't stand it.' Her mother said, 'Why are you glad you can't stand it?' 'Well,' said the girl, 'if I liked it I'd eat it all the time, and that would be terrible because I can't stand the stuff.'

A man went into a florist and said, 'Give me a bunch of flowers. I don't care what they are, just give me anything.' 'Do you want them scented?' the florist asked. And the man said, 'No, I'll take them with me.'

A termite at the local tip was eating a videotape of a movie. Another termite said, 'Is that any good?' And the first termite said, 'It's okay but the book was better.'

A man went up to a chicken and said, 'Cross the road.' And the chicken said. 'Why?'

A girl photocopied a mirror. Now she has two photocopiers.

Knock Three Times

Knock knock.
Who's there?
Barbara.
Barbara who?
Barbara black
sheep, have you
any wool?

Knock knock.
Who's there?
Butcher.
Butcher who?
Butcher left foot in, butcher left foot out . . .

Knock knock.
Who's there?
Baby owl.
Baby owl who?
Baby owl see you later, baby I won't.

Knock knock.
Who's there?
Toulouse.
Toulouse who?
Toulouse all that fat you'll need lots of exercise.

Knock knock.
Who's there?
Duke.
Duke who?
Duke come here often?

Knock knock.
Who's there?
Victor.
Victor who?
Victor his pants climbing over your fence.

Knock knock.
Who's there?
Pooch.
Pooch who?
Pooch your arms around me and give me a big kiss.

Knock knock.
Who's there?
Bumble bee.
Bumble bee who?
Bumble bee cold if you don't pull up your pants.

Knock knock.
Who's there?
Cook.
Cook who?
Stop doing bird impressions and let me in.

Knock knock.
Who's there?
Yah.
Yah who?
Ride 'em, cowboy!

Knock knock.
Who's there?
Ida.
Ida who?
I'd an idea you were going to say that.

Knock knock.
Who's there?
Lionel.
Lionel who?
Lionel roar if you stand on his tail.

Knock knock.
Who's there?
Frances.
Frances who?
France's north of Spain and south of Germany.

Knock knock.
Who's there?
Courtney.
Courtney who?
Courtney good movies recently?

Knock knock.
Who's there?
Phillip.
Phillip who?
Phillip my glass, I'm thirsty.

Knock knock.
Who's there?
Alison.
Alison who?
Alison to pop music, how about you?

Robustious Riddles

Ha, Ha, Ha!

*Tell them you'll stop
reading these riddles
when someone gets a
right answer!*

Why did the librarian have her hair in a bun?

Because she had her face in a hamburger.

Where can you buy fish eggs?

At a spawn shop.

Why did the termites stop working?

They thought it was boring.

What did the termite say when he left the tree?

It's been nice gnawing you.

What are a dentist's favourite two letters?

DK.

What does an educated owl say?

Whoooooooooom.

What do you do with a dog that chases everyone on a bicycle?

Take his bicycle away.

Why did the girl put sugar in her pyjamas?

She wanted to have sweet dreams.

What goes *dit dit dit da da squeak*?

  Mouse code.

What goes, 'Oh, oh, oh'?

  Santa Claus walking backwards.

How do you get a one-armed man out of a tree?

  Wave at him.

Where do geologists go for fun?

  To rock concerts.

Why did the chicken cross the playground?

  To get to the other slide.

How do you get rid of a boomerang?

Throw it down a one-way street.

What do you call a crazy spaceman?

An astronut.

What's an alien's favourite game?

Astronoughts and crosses.

What is the name for the science of shopping?

Buy-ology.

What has a bottom at the top?

Your legs.

Where does the queen keep her armies?

Up her sleevies.

Why are authors strange?

Because their tales (tails) come out of their heads.

Why didn't the fullback want to get on the plane?

He was scared the coach would put him on the wing.

Why isn't it safe to go to sleep on a train?

Because trains run over sleepers.

Why are football stadiums always cool?

Because they're full of fans.

What sweet little girl tells dirty jokes to wolves?

Little Rude Riding Hood.

What did one eye say to the other eye?

There's something between us and it smells.

What kind of plants are good in dark places?

Bulbs.

What happened to the butcher who backed into the meat slicer?

He got a little behind in his business.

What did the tie say to the hat?

You go on a head, I'll just hang around.

Why didn't the viper viper nose?

Because the adder adder handkerchief.

The Adder ad er andkerchief!

More Insults, More Injuries

He's so crooked he has to screw his socks on.

She's just a little girl, after all — after all she can get.

He gets really stroppy when you get to NO him.

She likes being tickled under the chin — all of them.

He's so old that when he went to school they didn't teach History — it hadn't started yet.

They call her 'The Dressmaker' because she makes so many slips.

They call her 'Parole' because she always interrupts people in the middle of a sentence.

They call him 'The Tunnel' because hi's such a big bore.

She's so old that when they told her to act her age she died.

He couldn't carry a tune if it had handles.

She's twelve years old going on all the time.

He's got a chip on his shoulder. Not surprising when you think that there's wood higher up.

She wins a lot of arguments but not many friends.

As a student, he's gone far. Unfortunately, not far enough.

She looks like she puts on her make-up with a paint roller.

He knows his own mind — which isn't saying much.

She's so ugly that she has to spend four hours at the beauticians — and that's just for an estimate.

Don't ever tell him a joke with a double meaning because he won't get either of them.

She's got a pretty little head. For a head, it's pretty little.

You couldn't call him a quitter — he always gets the sack before he can quit.

He's a self-made man. It's a pity he left out all the working parts.

She only makes friends with girls who have the same interests as she does — her.

He's money-mad. He can never make any money and it makes him mad.

There's a lot less to her than meets the eye.

She looks like a million — years.

Riotous Reading

Parachuting for Beginners by Hugo First

The Perfect Breakfast by Chris P. Bacon

Solitary Confinement by I. Malone

Late for School by Misty Buss

Talking to Parrots by L. O. Kocky

The Itchy Scalp by Dan Druff

Bank Robbing for Beginners by Anne Dover Deloot

The Selby Books by Trudy Light

A Visit to a Cathedral by Neil Downe

I Feel a Breeze by Isadore Open

I Caught a Cold by Anita Blow

Arctic Swimming for Beginners by I. C. Watters

Midnight Storm by Rainier Knight

Getting Rich Quickly by Dawn B. Leavitt

I Missed the Goal! by Hugh Blewitt

Auto Theft by Nick McCarr

How to be Helpful by Linda Hand

Buying Old Furniture by Anne Teake

Diary of a Criminal by Robyn Steele

My Weight Problem by I. Eta Lotte

Keeping Secrets by Betty Wont

Blabbing Secrets by U. Betty Will

In Trouble at School by C. Mee Layda

Listening to Songs by Anita Singh

Is School a Prison? by Midas Welby

A Wiggle Of Wriggles

A teacher asked a boy, 'Have you ever thought of going to the dentist to have your teeth checked?' And the boy said, 'No, I think I'd like to keep them white.'

A boy took the neighbour's dog for a walk and when he returned the neighbour was horrified. 'What have you done to him?' she screamed. 'He's all round and fat — he looks like a balloon.' 'Well, you told me to take him out for some air so I took him to a service station.'

A girl was running around and around the block. A police officer called out, 'What are you doing?' 'I'm running away from home,' the girl called back, 'only I'm not allowed to cross the street.'

A girl said to her friend, 'You must have been nervous when you asked for more pocket money.' 'No, I wasn't,' said her friend, 'I was calm and collected.'

A car broke down by the side of the road and a sheep came up to the driver's side of the car and said, 'Judging from the noise your car made I think you'll find that your timing gear is broken.'

The shocked driver watched as the sheep rejoined the mob and walked away. Soon a farmer came along and the driver of the car told him what had happened. 'Was it a sheep with a bit of a tear out of his ear?' 'Yes!' exclaimed the driver. 'That was him!' 'Well, I wouldn't pay any attention,' the farmer said, 'that's Ralph and he doesn't know a thing about cars.'

The art teacher looked at the drawing the girl was making. 'What's that?' she asked. 'It's a big fish eating a little fish,' the girl said. 'Where's the little fish?' the teacher asked. 'The big fish ate him,' the girl said. 'Then where's the big fish?' the teacher asked. 'He left,' the girl said. 'Would you hang around if there was nothing more to eat?'

A boy was lying in bed and he said to his mother, 'I can't go to sleep. My feet are freezing.' 'For heaven's sake,' his mother said, 'they're sticking out from under the covers. Pull them in.' 'Are you kidding,' the boy said, 'I'm not having those cold things in bed with me!'

A fisherman was carrying a fish. Another fisherman said, 'Where are you going?' The first fisherman said, 'I'm taking this fish home for dinner.' Suddenly the fish looked up and said, 'I've already eaten. Could we go to a movie instead?'

A girl went over to her friend's house and asked, 'Are your blinds drawn?' And the other girl said, 'No, they're real.'

A woman asked a man, 'Where's the money you owe me?' And the man said, 'Listen to this, the most fascinating thing happened to me today. My lucky number is nine and I just happened to wake up at nine o'clock. I looked outside and saw nine birds in a tree and nine cars parked in my street. So I went to a race meeting and put all my money on the ninth horse in race nine.' 'Did it win?' the woman asked. 'No,' said the man, 'it finished ninth.'

A man went into a restaurant and said, 'I'll have a lamb chop burnt to a crisp, some mushy carrots, and a salad with sand in it.' And the waiter said, 'I can't serve you that!' And the man said, 'Why not, that's what you gave me yesterday.'

A man was sitting on a park bench telling himself jokes and then laughing. Then, instead of laughing at a joke, he said, 'That's terrible!' Someone sitting nearby said, 'Why did you say, "That's terrible" after that joke?' And the first man said, 'Because I've heard it before.'

A girl said to her mother, 'Mum, quick! What time is it? I was invited to a party but my watch isn't going.' And her mother said, 'Why wasn't your watch invited too?'

A frog was double-parked on a lily pad. He was toad away.

A boy tried to get into Magic School. 'What magic can you do?' the headmaster asked. 'Can you turn a handkerchief into a bunch of flowers?' 'No,' said the boy, 'but I can walk down the street and turn into a laneway.'

One magician said to another magician, 'Whatever happened to that girl you used to saw in half?' 'She's very well,' said the first magician, 'she lives in Melbourne . . . and Brisbane.'

'Have you watched that new kids' TV show?' a girl asked her friend. 'I've watched it off and on,' her friend said. 'How did you like it?' the first girl said. 'Off,' her friend said.

A sign in the window of a house: 'Violin for sale.' A sign in the window of the house next door: 'Hooray!'

The Worst Cheapskate I Ever Knew

A stand-up comedy routine by Gary Gaggs

I knew this kid who was such a cheapskate that you wouldn't believe it. He had the shortest arms and the deepest pockets I've ever heard of. He was so tight-fisted that when he shook hands he only used one finger.

He was so tight that when he blinked, his kneecaps moved.

He once went on a week's holiday and all he spent was seven days.

He was always the first to put his hand in his pocket — and keep it there.

The teacher asked him if he was free after school and he said, 'No, but I'm reasonable.'

To make his glasses last longer he took them off when he wasn't looking at anything.

He was the sort of kid that if he paid you a compliment he'd ask for a receipt.

When someone said, 'Three cheers!' he only gave two.

He always had his nose in a book. He was too cheap to buy a handkerchief.

The only thing he ever gave away was a secret.

He asked a tailor if he could make him some pants with one-way pockets.

But seriously, folks, his pockets were the last part of his pants to wear out.

Later on I heard that he was going to get married. He hired a brass band for the wedding. He was going to put it on his bride's finger.

But seriously, folks, he almost cancelled the wedding when he found out that the price of confetti had gone up.

He wanted to save money on his honeymoon so he went alone.

For her birthday he gave his wife a fifty-piece dinner set — a box of toothpicks.

He once found a sling and broke his arm so he could use it.

To save money on sugar he keeps a fork in his sugar bowl.

Now he and his wife have kids. Every year he tears the December page off the calendar so the kids won't know when it's Christmas.

But seriously, folks, these days money is the last thing he thinks of — just before he goes to sleep.

Thank you for being such a great audience! I'd love to take you home with me — of course, it'll cost you.

Rickety
Riddles

I love riddles!

Why didn't the skeleton go to the dance?

Because he had no body to go with.

Why didn't the skeleton play church music?

Because he had no organs.

What did the monster wear to bed?

A fright-gown.

Who is a vampire most likely to fall in love with?

The girl necks door.

What would you get if you crossed a monster with a pair of trousers?

Scaredy pants.

How do monsters keep their hair in place?

With scare-spray.

What do sea monsters eat?

Fish and ships.

What do you call a skeleton that sleeps in?

Lazy bones.

Who did the monster take to the dance?

His ghoul-friend.

What do you call monsters who work on aeroplanes?

Fright attendants.

What did the skeleton order in the restaurant?

A glass of milk and a mop.

What position does a monster play on a soccer team?

Ghoulie.

What is Dracula's favourite ice cream?

Vein-illa.

What do you call a mummy who eats biscuits in bed?

A crummy mummy.

What should you take if a monster invites you to dinner?

Someone who runs slower than you do.

What do you call a nervous witch?

A twitch.

Why do cannibals make good police officers?

They love to grill suspects.

Why don't cannibals like to eat comedians?

They taste funny.

What is the cannibals' favourite game?

Swallow the leaders.

What is a monster's favourite game?

Hide and Shriek.

Where do baby monsters go when their parents are at work?

The day-scare centre.

Which day of the week is a cannibal's favourite day?

Chewsday.

Which day of the week is a ghost's favourite day?

Moan-day.

What do you do if a monster rolls his eyes at you?

Pick them up and roll them back.

Why do cannibals like athletes?

They like fast food.

What happened to the monster who ate Christmas decorations?

He got tinselitis.

What is a monster's favourite bedtime story?

Ghoul Deluxe and the Three Scares.

Why couldn't the boy vampire get a girlfriend?

He had bat breath.

What kind of music do mummies like best?

Wrap music.

A Fiddle of Fads

I can't stop laughing!

A woman dragged a boy into a doctor's office, screaming, 'Doctor, my son just swallowed a bullet! What should I do?' And the doctor said, 'I don't know but don't point him at me!'

A boy came into his friend's house, clutching his arm and asked. 'Did you say that your dog's bark is worse than his bite?' His friend said, 'Yes, why?' The first boy said, 'Whatever you do, don't let him bark because he just bit me and it was terrible!'

'Teacher, teacher!' the girl said. 'There was a turtle on the highway!' 'What was a turtle doing on the highway?' the teacher asked. 'About one kilometre an hour,' the girl answered.

'Aren't you a fast runner?' the gym teacher asked the girl. 'Yes, and no,' the girl said. 'What exactly is that supposed to mean?' the teacher asked. 'Well,' said the girl, 'it means just what I said: yes, I'm not a fast runner.'

'My friend's mother put on lots and lots of sun-block and now she's black and blue,' a girl told her mother. 'Really, darling,' her mother said, 'why do you suppose that is?' 'Simple,' said the girl, 'she slid off her beach chair.'

Two termites were eating their way through a house. One of them suddenly stopped and said to the other one, 'I'm exhausted. Let's take a coffee table break.'

A man said to his doctor, 'Suddenly I have a terrible memory. I can't remember anything.' The doctor said, 'How long has this been going on?' And the man said, 'How long has what been going on?'

'But teacher,' the boy said. 'You said you could teach me piano in ten easy lessons.' 'Well, yes,' the teacher said. 'But in your case you'll need about a hundred lessons before then.'

A sandwich walked into a bar and asked for a drink and the bartender said, 'I'm sorry but we don't serve food in here.'

A boy walked by a very very posh and expensive restaurant which had a sign in the window that said, 'We have every kind of food in the world! If we don't have what you want, we'll give you one thousand dollars.' The boy decided to make some money so he went in and a very snooty waiter found him a table. 'And what will sir be ordering today,' he asked. The boy quickly said, 'I'll have an elephant's ear on a bun.' 'An elephant's ear on a bun?' cried the waiter. 'Is that your order?' 'Yes,' said the boy, already thinking of the thousand dollars he was about to make. 'Will that be an African elephant or an Indian elephant?' the waiter said. 'Ah ... er ... African,' the boy said. 'Very well, sir, I'll have it for you in a jiffy. That is an excellent choice. The most expensive item we serve but you will love it.' The boy quickly looked around for a way to escape from the restaurant. He was tiptoeing towards a back door, when the waiter stood in his way. 'Here's your one thousand dollars, sir,' the man said, handing the boy the money. 'You mean you don't have any African elephant ears?' And the waiter said, 'No, we have plenty of them — but we're all out of buns.'

'All right, children,' the teacher said, 'which month has twenty-eight days?' A girl at the back of the room called out, 'They all do.'

A ship carrying a load of purple paint and a load of red paint ran into a desert island. The captain and crew were marooned.

Dino-Sores

What kind of game would a Brontosaurus play with people?

Squash.

How do you raise an orphaned Tyrannosaurus?

With a forklift.

How do you find out if a dinosaur is carnivorous or vegetarian?

Lie down on its plate.

Why did the dinosaur cross the road?

Because chickens weren't around yet.

What do you call a blind dinosaur?

Idontthinkhesaurus.

What do you call a five metre tall Brontosaurus?

Shorty.

How do you make a dinosaur stew?

Keep him waiting for an hour.

What's the best way to talk to a Tyrannosaurus.

Long distance.

What did the dinosaur say when the volcano blew up?

Have a lava-ly day.

What's green and sticky and hangs from tall trees?

Brontosaurus snot.

What do you do if you find a Tyrannosaurus in your bed?

Sleep somewhere else.

Where would you expect to find a dead dinosaur?

Wherever you left it.

Why did Brontosauruses have such long necks?

Because they had smelly feet.

What do you call a dinosaur driving a racing car?

A pronto bronto.

Knock till you Drop

I think I'm going to split my sides!

Knock knock.
Who's there?
Cows.
Cows who?
Cows go *moo*, not *hoo*.

Knock knock.
Who's there?
Ida.
Ida who?
Ida thought you could at least say please.

Knock knock.
Who's there?
Emma.
Emma who?
Emma your new neighbour — could I borrow
a cup of sugar?

Knock knock.
Who's there?
Cash.
Cash who?
I always thought
you were a nut.

Knock knock.
Who's there?
Juno.
Juno who?
Juno who it is?

Knock knock.
Who's there?
Mike.
Mike who?
Mike candle's just gone out and I'm standing in the dark.

Knock knock.
Who's there?
Miniature.
Miniature who?
Miniature you let me in I'll tell you who I am.

Knock knock.
Who's there?
Lou.
Lou who?
Lou's not working, can I use yours?

Knock knock.
Who's there?
Kiki.
Kiki who?
Kiki's not w-working and I'm f-freezing out here!

Knock knock.
Who's there?
Major.
Major who?
Major open the door, didn't I?

Knock knock.
Who's there?
Mariel.
Mariel who?
Mariel name is a secret.

Knock knock.
Who's there?
Cameron.
Cameron who?
Cameron film are what you need to take photos.

Knock knock.
Who's there?
Felix.
Felix who?
Felix my ice cream, I'll be furious!

Knock knock.
Who's there?
Rice Bubbles.
Rice Bubbles who?
I'll tell you tomorrow — it's a cereal.

Knock knock.
Who's there?
Wilma.
Wilma who?
Wilma life ever be free from these knock knock jokes?!

My nature Walk

HA HA HA!

A stand-up
comedy routine
by Gary Gaggs

I went for a drive through one of those zoos where the animals are all around and the people stay in these little vans. It was just me and the guide in my van and it turns out he used to be a comedian. 'You're Gary Gaggs, aren't you?' he said. 'That's me,' I admitted, 'what's your name?' He said, 'My name's Ralph and I'm very glad it is.' I said, 'Why are you glad that your name is Ralph?' And he said, 'Because that's what everybody calls me.'

I said, 'You mean you were a comedian and you gave it up to become a guide in a zoo?' And he said, 'No, I used to also be a tree-surgeon but one day I fell out of a patient.'

Anyway, the van broke down and we had to walk back. 'It's perfectly safe,' he said, 'I know all about these animals.' So, we were walking along near some rhinos and I was getting kind of nervous. So I said to him, 'What happens if one of them charges us?' He said, 'I don't think we should pay him a cent.' That's what he said.

He said, 'You don't know a lot about animals, do you?' And I said, 'No, not a lot.' And he said, 'I'll give you a quiz: I have a trunk in the middle

of my face, two huge ears and wrinkly skin. What am I?' And I said, 'Extremely ugly.'

Anyway, we saw a herd of elephants. Magnificent animals. After a minute I turned to the guide and said, 'Why is their skin so wrinkly?' And he said, 'Have you ever tried to iron one?'

So I said, 'Seriously, what steps do we take if they come after us?' And he said, 'I don't know about you but I'll be taking blinkin' great huge ones — and lots of them.' That's what he said.

He said, 'At this time of year, elephants are on the move. But it takes them a long time to get going.' 'Why's that?' I asked. And he said, 'Because they have to pack their trunks.' (I did say he *used* to be a comedian.)

I saw this big orange-coloured parrot in a tree. So I asked, 'What kind of parrot is that orange one over there?' And he said, 'I call it a carrot.' Seriously, that's what he said.

So there was this crocodile lying on the riverbank. We got up close and the guy whispered, 'They make good pets, you know.' 'Do they really?' I said. And he said, 'Yes, they don't eat much and they're very fond of little children.' (This guy was starting to get on my nerves.)

Anyway, I told him that I'd once seen a whole herd of a kind of deer that are totally blind. 'Totally blind?' he said. 'What kind of deer were they?' And I said, 'No idea.' Get it? 'No-eye-deer.' That fixed him.

'Are there any leopards around here?' I asked. 'Yes,' he said, but we can't find them ever since we used spot remover on them.'

I said to him, I said, 'Have you ever heard of a twip?' And he said, 'No, what's a twip?' And I said, 'A twip is what a wabbit takes on a twain.'

I said to the guide, 'When do lion cubs start to hunt?' And he said, 'First of all, the lioness gives them some advice.' I said, 'What kind of advice?' And he said, 'Don't cross the road till you see the zebra crossing.'

Then we saw a snake with a cold. I knew she had a cold because she had to viper nose.

I said to him, 'Look out! There's a deadly snake curled around your foot!' And he said, 'Which foot?'

I said, 'Do you ever get any poachers here?' And he said, 'As a matter of fact, I'm a poacher myself.

I poached a couple of eggs this morning for breakfast.'

So I said, 'No, not that kind of poacher. I mean the kind who steals animals.' And he said, 'There was a guy who stole a very rare wild pig about a week ago but we caught him.' I said, 'How'd you catch him?' And he said, 'The pig squealed.'

The poacher had built a very tall building to keep all of his stolen pigs in. He called it a *sty-scraper*.

The guide said, 'There were these guys who used to sneak down to the ocean at night to catch octopuses and hold them for ransom.' I said, 'Really?' And he said, 'Yes, they were *squid-nappers*.'

I said, 'What kind of bird is that one over there? The one that looks like it's out of breath.' And he said, 'I guess it's a puffin.'

That's when he fell into a waterhole. I think his glasses prescription had just ran out.

Then we came to a tree covered in termites, only the termites weren't doing anything. I said, 'Why aren't they getting into that tree?' And he said, 'Because it's boring work.'

I said, 'But seriously, why aren't they?' And he said, 'Stop bugging me.'

I saw a flea on my arm and I was about to flick it off when he said, 'Don't do that!' I said, 'Why not?' And he said, 'The poor little thing is just *itch-hiking*.'

I flicked it off and was about to get rid of another one when he said, 'That one doesn't look like it's up to scratch.'

I can't get enough of Gary's gags!

He said, 'Do you know the difference between a coyote and a flea?' And I said, 'No, what's the difference between a coyote and a flea?' And he said, 'One howls on the prairie and the other one prowls on the hairy.' That's what he said.

We crossed this little stream and he fell in. Then he jumped up and said, 'Ding dong, ding dong.' And I said, 'What are you saying that for?' And he said, 'I'm wringing wet.'

There was this tall bird standing in the water on one leg. We crept closer and closer to have a better look and I said, 'Why is it standing on one leg?' And he said — do you know what he said? — he said, 'Because if it lifted the other one it would fall down.' (He got me there.)

That's when I stepped on something brown and sticky. You guessed it: it was a stick.

Thank you, you're the greatest!

Boomerangs

I'm very open-minded.
You ought to be because there's nothing in it.

Last weekend I went to the zoo.
Really? Which cage did they put you in?

I've got an idea.
It must be beginner's luck.

I've just changed my mind.
I hope the new one works better than the old one.

She's a real saint.
And she looks like one too: a Saint Bernard.

She's as pretty as a flower.
Yes, a cauliflower.

I'm watching my weight.
Go up and up and up . . .

He's got a mind of his own.
Well, who else would want it?

And to think that she started out with nothing.
Yes, and she's still got most of it.

He's got a baby face.
So he does — and a brain to match it.

Those two make a great pair.
That's true — she's a headache and he's a pill.

Have you been talking to yourself?
No, why?
Because you look bored.

A faddle of fiddles

These are a
hoot!

The school bully fell off his bike and was lying on the footpath. Another boy came along and the bully said, 'Help! Call me an ambulance!' And the other boy said, 'Okay, you're an ambulance.'

The class went to the new swimming centre. 'All right, children,' the swimming teacher said. 'The pool over there is for good swimmers and that shallow one is for beginners.' One of the kids looked at an empty pool nearby that was being cleaned. 'How about that one?' he asked. 'Is that for kids who can't swim?'

A pirate captain wanted to buy some earrings but he didn't want to pay any more than a buccaneer.

A murderer was about to be hanged. 'Do you have a last request?' the warder asked him. 'Yes, I'd like to sing a song.' 'Okay, go ahead.' 'Row row row your boat, gently down the stream, merrily merrily merrily merrily, life is but a dream. Row row row your boat, gently down the stream, merrily merrily merrily merrily, life is but a dream. Row row row your boat, gently down the stream, merrily merrily merrily merrily, life is but a dream . . . '

A boy threw a bucket of paint at his sister and it splattered all across the lounge-room wall. His mother chased him around the house, screaming, 'I'll teach you to throw buckets of paint at your sister!' And the boy said, 'I wish you would — I missed her completely!'

A woman ordered a cup of tea in a cafe and then had to go to the loo before she could finish it. She looked around and wondered if anyone would drink the rest of it while she was away from her table. Suddenly she had an idea: she wrote a note on her serviette and put it next to the cup of tea. It said, 'Don't drink this tea, I spat in it.' When she came back from the loo, the tea was still there but someone had written on the note, 'So did I.'

A boy and a girl were watching big waves crash on the beach. For a moment it was calm and then a tiny wave came in. 'Look,' said the girl, 'a microwave!'

A woman went to see a friend who had just had a baby. The friend was listening to the baby and writing things on a piece of paper. 'What are you doing?' the woman asked. The new mother said, 'When he gets bigger I'm going to ask him what he meant.'

A cat was doing her morning exercises. She was doing puss-ups.

Then there were the swimmers who left the water because the sea weed.

A man was sitting on a park bench, eating lunch, when a woman came along walking her dog. The dog raced up and started snapping at the man's sandwiches. He pulled them out of the way and said to the woman, 'Do you mind if I throw him a bit?' 'Not at all,' the woman said, smiling. With this the man picked up the dog and threw him over the fence.

A shark went to the dentist and the dentist said, 'What's all this stuff stuck between your teeth?' And the shark said, 'Slow fish.'

'Let's have a party on deck tonight,' the boy said to the girl on the cruise ship. 'Yes, but where on deck?' the girl asked. And the boy answered, 'I'll be where the funnel be.'

A tortoise was robbed by a snail. The police came and asked what the snail looked like and the tortoise said, 'I don't know. It all happened so fast.'

The lighthouse keeper bought some hens so that he could have eggs with his beacon.

A woman went into a butcher shop and saw a dog waiting at the counter. 'How much mince do you need today?' the butcher asked. The dog barked twice and the butcher wrapped up two kilos of mince. Then the butcher said, 'And how many sausages today?' The dog barked four times and the butcher wrapped up four sausages. The dog went off down the street with the parcels in his mouth and the woman followed to see where he was going. The dog pressed his nose against the doorbell and when a man opened the door the woman said, 'That's a very clever dog you have.' 'You've got to be joking,' the man said, 'this is the third time this week he's forgotten his key.'

a giggle of riddles

Why did the monster stand on his head?

He was turning things over in his mind.

How does a monster cure a sore throat?

He gargoyles.

How do you talk to a giant?

Use big words.

What do you call a hairy beast that's lost?

A where-wolf.

Why did the witch have trouble singing?

Because she had a frog in her throat.

What did the monster do when he lost his hand?

He went to the second hand shop.

What does a witch do when her broom slams on the brakes?

She flies off the handle.

When is it bad luck to see a black cat?

When you're a mouse.

What do motorised witches fly around on?

Brooooooooom sticks.

Why do black cats try to sing?

They think they're mewsical.

What kind of dogs do vampires like?

Bloodhounds.

How can a witch live on garlic alone?

If you lived on garlic, you'd live alone too.

'Goodness me,' the auntie monster said when she saw a leg sticking out of her nephew's head, 'you've grown a foot since I saw you last.'

What do ghosts wear when they go hiking?

Booooooots!

When a robot dies, what do they write on its grave?

Rust in peace.

What goes *cackle cackle cackle clunk*?

A witch laughing her head off.

What goes *boo hoo plop boo hoo plop*?

A witch crying her eyes out.

What do witches do best at in school?

Spelling.

What do you call a skeleton that's been hit over the head?

A numbskull.

What do snakes write at the bottom of their letters?

Love and hisses.

Welcome to the Academy awarts!

What kind of prizes do witches get?

Academy awarts.

How many witches does it take to change a light globe?

Only one, but she changes it into a toad.

Why did the vampire cross the road?

Because it was attached to the chicken's neck.

What does a baby zombie want for her birthday?

A deady bear.

What do you call a team of vultures playing soccer?

Foul play.

Why did the monster catch centipedes?

He wanted scrambled legs for breakfast.

Why did the monster eat the streetlight?

He only wanted a light meal.

What did the cannibal ask the waiter for on the cruise ship?

The passenger list.

Why are skeletons always calm?

Because nothing gets under their skin.

Who won the vampires' race?

No one. They finished neck and neck.

What did the monster say when she ate a herd of gnus?

'. . . And that's the end of the gnus.'

Knock It Off!

Knock knock.
Who's there?
Panther.
Panther who?
My panther falling down, pleathe open the door.

Knock knock.
Who's there?
Troy.
Troy who?
Troy as I might, I can't reach the doorbell.

Knock knock.
Who's there?
Wayne.
Wayne who?
Wayne, Wayne go away, come again another day.

Knock knock.
Who's there?
Army.
Army who?
Army and you still friends?

Knock knock.
Who's there?
Ice cream soda.
Ice cream soda who?
Ice cream soda whole neighbourhood will wake up!

Knock knock.
Who's there?
Tick.
Tick who?
Tick 'em up, I'm a wobber!

Knock knock.
Who's there?
Madame.
Madame who?
Madame hand is sore from knocking.

Knock knock.
Who's there?
Amin.
Amin who?
Amin, so don't bother opening the door.

Knock knock.
Who's there?
Nana.
Nana who?
Knock knock.
Who's there?
Nana.
Nana who?
Knock knock.
Who's there?
Aunt.
Aunt who?
Aunt you glad that Nana's gone away?

Knock knock.
Who's there?
Ammonia.
Ammonia who?
Ammonia poor girl and nobody loves me.

Knock It Off!

Knock knock.
Who's there?
Furry.
Furry who?
Furry's a jolly good fellow, furry's a jolly good
fellow . . .

Knock knock.
Who's there?
Kermit.
Kermit who?
Kermit a crime and you'll go to jail.

Knock knock.
Who's there?
Waiter.
Waiter who?
Waiter minute while I tie my shoelace.

Knock knock.
Who's there?
Police.
Police who?
Police stop telling me
these terrible knock
knock jokes!

YOU'RE BEAUTIFUL

One day I want to learn Gary's 'killer joke', the one that landed everyone in hospital. The problem is Gary won't tell it anymore and the people who know it can't tell it because they start laughing so hard they can't get the words out.

Anyway I hope you liked these jokes. If you were sad, I hope you're happy now. I know I am.

So, as Gary always says...

You're beautiful,

Selby

ABOUT THE AUTHOR

Duncan Ball is an Australian author and scriptwriter best known for his popular books for children. Among his most-loved works are the ten collections of stories about Selby the talking dog.

His other books include the Emily Eyefinger series about the adventures of Emily Eyefinger (who was born with an eye on the end of her finger), three books about the diabolical tricks of a cunning and cranky ghost, and two books about Bert Piggott: *Piggott Place* and *Piggotts in Peril*.

Duncan lives in Sydney with his wife, Jill, and their comical cat, Jasper. As far as Duncan knows, his cat can't talk. But Jasper still somehow manages to get everyone to do exactly as he wants.

For more information about Selby and Emily and Bert and Duncan's other books surf your way to Selby's web site at: **www.harpercollins.com.au/selby**